ABOUT THE AUTHOR

Hannah Swingler is a poet, teacher and artist, born and bred in Birmingham. She calls a forward roll a 'gambole'.

She was the winner of CoachesSLAM 2018, as well as coaching the University of Birmingham's uniSLAM team to victory. She went on to represent the UK at CUPSI in Philadelphia.

She has performed across the country: with Tongue Fu, featuring at Howl, Grizzly Pear, , Verve Poetry Festival, Cafe Grande Slam, Stirchley Speaks, and at REP Birmingham, BOM, the Old REP, Ikon Gallery, Upstairs at the Western, Derby Theatre, Oxjam Fest, Birmingham Weekender and mac, amongst others. She featured on BBC radio discussing the importance of poetry for young people.

Hannah is an alumnus of both the National Youth Theatre of Great Britain and Beatfreeks YSC.

She believes good things come to those who make.

Twitter: @HannahSwings
www.facebook.com/hannswings
https://hannahswings.com

Hannah Swingler
This dress has pockets

VERVE
POETRY PRESS
BIRMINGHAM

PUBLISHED BY VERVE POETRY PRESS
Birmingham, West Midlands, UK
https://vervepoetrypress.com
mail@vervepoetrypress.com

FIRST PUBLISHED JAN 2019

Printed and bound in the UK
by TJ International, Padstow

ISBN: 978-1-912565-11-5

Cover art by Ceren Kilic

For June and Eileen -
The powerhouse women
who always stole the show.

CONTENTS

Hannah Introduces *Jess Davies, Asim Khan, Hannah Ledlie and Dennis Nkurunziza.*

Acknowledgements

This dress has pockets

Freddie Mercury

When I am nine, my parents move us to the countryside, away from bus routes and gang wars. The house they buy is bigger, too cheap for what it offers and their deliberation doesn't last long. They don't think to look at the old wiring; block out the sound of the motorway at the bottom of the garden.
Financial recklessness is hereditary.

We continue to go to school in the city, work in the city: be city dwellers that must sleep where we can see the stars clearer. Thirteen miles there, another thirteen back: the car becomes our living room, our bedroom, our home.
It doesn't have a CD player, so my brother makes jukebox cassettes, one song per family member then repeat. I choose Jesus of Surburbia by Green Day because it is nine minutes and seven seconds long and I crave the attention.

Fields, trees, abandoned farm buildings, hair pin bends, blind junctions, I know the landscape better than the opening to my favourite movie.

I write birthday cards leaning on headrests without curving a line.
  I can apply a full face of makeup using the rear view mirror from the backseat.
     I learn to change outfits without flashing the driver.
      I devour books like they will be burnt at the end of the day.

My brother falls in love with a girl who lives opposite our school. He stays overnight on a camp bed in her living room, I think. He stops making mix tapes. I am given an ipod for my birthday and spend the mornings staring out of the window pretending I am in a music video.

My mother only drives when my Dad is already home. At night, she turns the lights off on roads without cat eyes and we scream in the seconds of darkness, before we flash back to visibility. One night, we drive passed a man in drag walking in the road towards us. Two weeks later, the local headlines talk of a "decapitated tranny" who got hit by a car on her way home from a dinner party.
My Mom stops turning the lights off after that.

Mornings mean minus six degrees and the heater breaks.

I fall in love with a boy who lives opposite my school in an adjacent road to my brother's girlfriend. I can see my art room from my bedroom window. I stay overnight on a camp bed, sometimes.
I'm not sure whether the reason I love him is because I get an extra half an hour of sleep in the morning.

We resurrect Freddie Mercury on a thunder filled October night through a dramatic, unrehearsed yet surprisingly harmonised word-perfect rendition of Bohemian Rhapsody. We congratulate each other on hitting the high notes, swerve to miss a pheasant and hit a tree instead.

When I graduate - after thirteen years of thirteen miles there and thirteen back - my parents move to the road my brother's now fiancée lives on. I can see my old art-room from my bedroom window. I get an extra half an hour of sleep in the morning.
There are bus routes and gang wars and no blind junctions.
We do not make mix tapes.
We do not resurrect Freddie Mercury anymore, but I can still apply liquid eyeliner travelling over potholes using the rear view mirror from the backseat.

Graze

The dust doesn't dance in the sunlight in your room
It's more like commuters alighting at rush hour
Already tired
Barely slept

The birds have been awake for hours, no nightfall here
They sing through their insomnia
I vow to disconnect the streetlamps
Hope they'll bring their nests closer

A train speeds under our apartment block
The bed frame shudders
Your leg is above the covers
No monster dares strike and disturb you

There is a scrap of batter shaped graze across your kneecap
I want to touch it, but I don't
I compare it to my poppy petal thin skin, translucent
Painted in gouache: an Egon Schiele prep sketch

I don't remember the last time I played so wildly I lost my
balance.

Your graze is starting to scab into rows of backstitch
The colour of undiluted squash
I bet it itches, I want to itch it
But I don't

I can smell the new soap I bought yesterday on your skin
Mixed in with sleep, with your eye crust
With the dust from the sheet
Not changed in weeks

I have never willed for a moment to lodge in my memory
Like seeing you so still
I want to photograph your scars
As proof that our bodies want us to keep going

Consciously, I run my fingers
Over the system of purple streams
Miles before they meet the estuary, littering my thighs
That I have always hated

Now, I whisper hello
Thank you
Keep going, please
Heal me if you have to

Today should be a Sunday
So I snooze the alarm
We'll just have to be late
I'm not ready to play out, just yet.

Inventory 1

- The grease soaked chip paper from two paper scollops, salted
- A full vacuum bag
- The first slice of bungy sponge
- A bar of soap indented with fingernail marks (milk and honey scented)
- The last Christmas card that was signed with both of their names
- 200 euros
- The syrup from a melted slush puppy dried sticky in the glove compartment
- The sweat gathered in the finger holes of a bowling ball
- A 20p mix up from Frank's on the corner (consisting only of jelly snakes)
- A sprinkle of talcum powder
- The hair balled from a hairbrush about to be thrown to the birds
- The latch from the hallway phone

Say my name

The first letter left first, or just didn't show

The last three the last to leave

The lilt of her voice

Greeting me, smiling

Vanished

Like a lisp

Like a night-time lightning storm

A little girl on a milk carton

But I just turned my back for a second.

I made a sign for the livingroom door

Had to change the start time because I've spent too long making
      the tickets
Glue and glitter litter the floor
As Dad drags his high blood pressure in over the threshold
Drags on his first cigarette before dinner
Mom grates cheese over instant mashed potato
And burns the pork chops just how he likes them.
I think of burning across my inner thighs
Muscle on fire
As my dance teacher sits on my back and I beg to become bendier
I don't understand why my legs have to be so far apart—

Dance show tonight

My brother lies across the floor as I attempt to practice:
Playing Crash Bandicoot, his socks half off.
I trace shapes into the carpet with my feet, twirl in front of the
      screen and
He curses my name like I've thrown his football over a mountain top

But there's a dance show on tonight and ITS NOT FAIR I NEED TO
      PRACTICE I'M GOING TO TELL

I steal my mom's makeup that smells how I think Princess Diana would
Blush like a warrior, too much
My fingers shimmer, don't linger as they're
Wiped on the side of my dress—
I want my mom to cut my fringe before I go on
But the noise of hair being chopped,
the scrunch of my eyes too late for the blade

THERE'S A DANCE SHOW ON TONIGHT AND NO ONE SEEMS
   TO HAVE NOTICED.

A showcase of last week's tournament
Where Mom let me wear her Scarlet Siren lipstick
The point now rounded like a popsicle stick half sucked
I'm holding a number, feet in first position
(Because I've become quite superstitious) Smile as wide as I can
Run my tongue across fillings after too many pick and mix dinners
Through the gaps in my grin
Imperfect equals deducted points
Scarlet siren is more a statement when kept shut.

there's a dance show on tonight

I did not place, again.
Lipstick shade wasn't right
Toes weren't fully pointed
Stomach shape wasn't right
Collarbone tips not fully pointed
My scalp scratched by hair grips, gelled back, head lice trapped
Thigh veins snapped from not warming up properly
"Drive on the footpath, skip the traffic. This is her first troupe piece
   and she's finally making friends."
I think of the wages spent on costumes I'll outgrow in a month
Of growing without being able to stop
Of pork fat next to room temperature baked bean juice and my
   insides on my outside
I think of the hunger
To be good enough
Aged nine.

DANCE SHOW TONIGHT

I've placed 'reserved' signs on the sofa cushions
In the places we always sit.
Tickets handed out
The cassette wound back.
They'll be here soon, surely.
I wait by the poster, feet in first position.
I've practiced my set: Whitney then Britney and REM
No pliez or box steps I will mostly spin, to be honest.)
At the end,
My family will applaud and shout 'encore'
And my mom will cover my face in Scarlet Siren kisses
My father will be so impressed he'll stop smoking
My brother will let me play
They'll tell me the night is mine to celebrate
We'll eat drive thru food as the victory meal
And I will finish every bite
Tonight

Like
popcorn
kernels stuck
in my teeth,
your love
distracts
from the plot
points

Teach me shorthand

He had said
We can send secret notes across the office
Pretend that we're classmates
Close enough to sleep over at each other's houses
Different beds on different floors
Of course

The language is dying, there is no point, he replied.
Then we should definitely do it.

He planned to spray paint

Across the bridge he drove under to work
So only he would notice

And after a night of too much talk
He had finally collapsed
Into the same bed on the same floor
Woken at 11:07 to a cold pillow
His coat off the hook
A note by the key bowl
Saying

Kingsway Picturehouse

I was born in a bath tub, one of seven.   Seven wonders of the world

and the centre of my mother's universe.
My father brought us up on Hollywood and   three jobs' wages
Bought us pebble shaped toffees   good enough to skim

    Agnosia
                    That I can still taste now.
That felt like silk against the sharp tongue of siblings
    nability to recognise objects by using the senses

The best days were Saturdays at   Kingsway Picturehouse
As I stared at the screen and ached for a   yellow brick road
In velvet seats   too heavy
and me   too light
The chair's hinges closed and I folded up
                Like a paper doll with split pin limbs.
My favourite was a lemon sherbet Sunday best dress
                Handed down and taken in at
                    the sides.
School days spent deciphering mathematical equation signs

Which might as well be   pauses

or   kisses

or   crucifixes

    Altered perception

Not a right or wrong answer

       You're wrong about her

Not black or white

    Grey matter

Silver screen

    With a sliver of a chance

           When I grow up, I want to be

    Amnesia

      Discharged without my permission

    Sectioned

         Wait, I --

I was born in a bath tub, one of seven.

       Now two.

         Two. Too. Too many.

    Too many variants to say.

       She's not usually like this.

         You're a liar.

    Lack of

       Good days

Saturdays -

    Now derelict.

    Communication impairment

        Picturehouse

        Too heavy.

    Looks how she feels.

Too light

    She never used to be like this.

        Sherbert dress

    You should consider putting her--

Digging into pockets

    Paranoia

        You stole it

    Sensory stimulation

        You're always stealing my

            things

Always sharing half with me.

        And I've had enough of it

        Honestly

        never

        never..

        nnn.nmn

         never

            Think.

Think!
Who do you think you are?
Who do you?
Who?
Who? ...

Who are you?

I think I'm

Take her house key
        Take her dignity
      Take her wedding ring
        I'll take her home

When I get her back.
    Not this.
  Not this.
Not this.

Frail
Confused
Frustrated
Lonely

Version
    Not a number
    Not an inpatient

Not crossed out paragraphs on scribbled through paperwork.
Not a blue forget-me-knot marketing campaign

I am not past

Present but

Possibly future

Possibly your future.

I am a person

person

With an impaired brain

But a warrior heart

And feet in slippers knocking my heels together

And I'm just trying

Trying

Tttt-rr

Trrrriiiii

I'm just trying to get back

home.

Blue is a colour

Between violet and green
On the optical spectrum of visible light.
Human eyes perceive blue
when observing light with a wavelength between
450 and 495 nanometres.
Blue is everywhere and everyone
In electronic RGB screens and every newborn's eyes.
It is also the colour of my anxiety.
Trickling towards oxygenation
Mixed in with adrenaline
Bleeding like hair in bathwater.
Blue is hidden in plain sight.
Between the sky and the ocean
And it's swirling like a cyclone
Before the tsunami hits.

Blue began as 8000 litres of water
To produce 1 pair of jeans
That pool around a father's ankles
Blue becomes 2 minutes and 2 parallel lines
On a stick in a public toilet
Appearing like dropped china
Onto a mother's five-year plan.
Blue is hereditary.
The most expensive pigment
But the most overlooked.
I'm the only girl, second born
And blue looks great on me.

It is the colour of loneliness
Whether its bottles of cheap gin
Emptied between friends
Or a single eared artist's insides.
Blue is the colour of wrong place, wrong time
The lips of a black boy
After blinking at a policeman's gun
Sirens and flashes
Spilling out of your record player on full volume
Blue is a colour
Some find difficult to see
Maybe because we're so used to seeing it.

Now don't get me wrong,
I'm not trapped in a Turner painting
I understand that blue is a primary colour,
And you need it to mix a spectrum
But I still have days
Trapped between the sunlight
With clouds of navy haze that choke up my lungs
When all I see is ink blots
Scarring blank pages meant to inspire.
Niggling feelings are dripping taps
Turn to flooded homes
And I can't be the only one
Unprepared for this sudden disaster.
I can't be the only one
Sleeping with the windows open
And whispering "Thank goodness" to the rain
So I have an excuse to not leave the house today.

But blue has too many shades
To colour between my lines using only one.
Use sapphire, cobalt and teal
Because peacocks stand proud of their hues
Use periwinkle, aqua and indigo,
Because I refuse to only be 'blue'.

Inventory 2

- A sponge soaked in the pigment of a favourite colour
- The batteries from the TV remote
- An ark of origami animals made from the doodled pages of a maths book
- The leftover milk in the bottom of a cereal bowl
- The top button of a blue linen shirt
- A collage of all the skies in the photos we've taken
- A cat's claw (3.4mm)
- A pack of fruit pastilles, the reds missing
- A jar of rain water from that evening
- A conker, unshelled
- The lead piping from a game of Cluedo (c.1960s)
- My contact lenses from 2009 onwards, trapped between glass slides

Good deed

You heard that sugar water would help
So you fill a milk lid at the tap
Mixed with caster sugar
Because that's all you had
Your fingertip tastes sweet now
As the bee sits on the slabs
Not flying
And you place the lid by the bee
And he walks away from it
Using all his energy, you can tell
And you think
For fucks sake, bee,
I'm trying to help you here

I left the dress you lent me in Spain

laid out on a deck chair.
Holidaymakers think someone came down from their room before
breakfast to claim the perfect space three years ago, near the shore-
line yet not too far from the bar. They're too polite to move it.
Instead they set up around it, watch the sleeves reach out in the
breeze as though giving them the finger. They complain to their
partners over paperbacks with broken spines and rub factor 5 across
their thighs. The partners nod and glance at the cotton, imagine it
dancing towards them, knowing exactly what it's doing, imagine it
puddled across the floorboards next to their partner's nightstand and-
I imagine the dress staring back, hoping it will be folded up and taken
somewhere else in a suitcase, amongst half empty bottles of stolen
shampoo and a carrier bag full of shells and crab carcasses that will
be forgotten on a back step. It misses the stillness of the suburbs, the
smell of your aloe vera sun cream skin.

I remember the first time that you wore it.
You didn't undo the zip and got it caught on your glasses, which fell
to the floor and gave you flashbacks to feeling useless whilst watching
Velma in Scooby Doo. You called my name over the changing room
wall like Officer Lightholler at the end of Titanic when he's in the
lifeboat with the torch and he's pushing frozen mothers away and
shouting: 'Is anyone alive out there?'. I open the changing room door
and squeeze in, your arms are trapped and you kind of look like those
inflatable tubes at American car washes and I tell you this and you
snort laugh and then say 'shit I think I just snotted on the dress' which
makes us laugh even more. When we finally work out the buttons, we
confirm that it makes your boobs look phenomenal and you decide to
spend even the money your Dad gave us for the bus ride home on it.
It rains, a summer downpour that makes the pavement change colour
twice within an hour but we share a cone of chips on the way home to

stay warm and I don't even mind that my new Converse are
drenched. You dare me to drink the vinegar at the bottom of the
cone and I do, an acidic singe in my throat. We go back to yours
and lie on your bed with our necks exposed, heads filling with blood
until we're woozy. We stretch out above the covers because it's so
humid and fall asleep talking about our secret getaway to anywhere
other than here. Where we might just stay, actually, burn the return
tickets on a beach campfire surrounded by people more glamorous
than us and eat and drink and drink and drink and swim.

I wrote you a letter after it happened.
It was during the epiphany phase that writers realise tears are salty
and so is the ocean and you become really good at water metaphors.
(I felt soaked down to the bone, my mouth drying at the taste of
your name. I vowed for my tears to taste sweet, poured salt-shakers
across tablecloths and sketched your name into them when dinner
wasn't quite over. Threw one handful over each shoulder because I
can never remember which side you told me the devil was waiting
on.)

I have a new friend who doesn't lend me dresses.
She says that my knees look like babies faces and maybe I should
think twice before showing them off. Instead, she tells me facts
about how all life originated in the oceans, and that we carry salt
water in our bodies because we cannot let go of where we came
from. Water metaphors sound better when she writes them. The
dress looked better on you. I couldn't have it hanging in my
wardrobe like a cotton blend phantom, it's bad enough feeling
haunted every time I pass a chip shop.
So it will stay in Spain where I travelled without you.
Shrinking every time the tide comes in.

Crown Shyness

At first, she had gone and back and forth about it, the pamphlet
on the doormat, stepped over all week. She had read, as her cereal
grew soggy, the spoon hovering just under her chin, the milk
dripping off.
Yes, she did believe in replanting the forest the estate had been
named after, giving the town a breath of fresh air, a sense of peace
not felt since

      Anyway,
             she applied; her interview blouse pulled from the
bottom of the washing pile, a solidified drop of chocolate perched
on her chest. She hoped they wouldn't notice, but decided she
didn't stand a chance since she was new to this whole technological
progression thing and everyone else in the waiting area had the
arrogance shrouded desperation of being newly graduated.
Her CV held a large hole that had pulled the last two years into it,
and when they asked, she blamed the machines for being quicker
than her at reporting, even though there had been a scandal since
about how the difference between 'hyper' and 'hypo' was not
recognised and some diagnoses had been misreported.

Her neck went red.

                 She had spent her redundancy
money on a trip to Barmouth, the days poured out watching the
estuary drift under the bridge, trying to prove to herself that
change was a good thing.
              But the money had trickled away too

Anyway,
she told the story of learning the names of each tree with her father
as a child, taping leaves onto sugar paper scrapbook pages and
drawing from them. A fist width sliver of silver birch bark was the
centrefold, of course

and before she realised what was happening, she
was shaking the interviewer's hand. He said he liked her organic
energy and believed her to be a good fit for the role and then made
a joke about a centrefold he favoured as a kid, which she wasn't
offended by until she was home, cooking gammon and egg for tea.

She didn't know what shoes to wear, so bought new hiking boots
from the city centre store and they rubbed her toes by 10:15am, her
fault for not breaking them in.

She had been surprised at how many doors had passcodes at the
entrance, apparently to stop vandals or dark tourists. No recording
equipment is allowed within the woods, this is a place of memorial,
not photo shoots, but she still felt it a shame that the general public
couldn't enjoy the space without a copy of a death certificate or a
staff badge.

As she walked the rows of trees, she imagined what the caskets were
like underground.
Not glowing, as first dreamt about, but like mermaid's purses, shark
foetuses squirming around.

She said 'good morning' to those walking in the woods, the regulars
who bring meals and left a plate behind at the roots, those hanging
handmade pompoms along the lower branches on birthdays and
anniversaries.

That day, she had received another complaint about the woodpecker nesting in PLOT472OAK3. Carving into the bark is prohibited after all, but sometimes during the weekly inspections, she'll find fresh initials. She knew she couldn't blame the woodpecker for that.

Since her days off, PLOT63ELM1 had been gifted a lilac scarf wrapped around its trunk, as though dropped from a pushchair and found by a stranger.
This tree's electronic data grid was only a fifth shaded in, maybe less than that. Her heart moaned, or she supposed that it did, and she tried not to think of how her data grid would look.
She imagined swiping to the 'quantities' page, to the number of blood cells and bad thoughts, listed amongst all the times that she had laughed or lied, felt complete wonder or all-consuming fear. Of how many heartbeats and kisses and dances and injuries and raised voices or arm hairs and backspaced messages and sleeps and dances and moments of undeniable love she had felt, tallied up.

She never went to the end of the document, the photo ID page made it difficult when Dutch Elm hit.

Anyway,
when she looked up, the branches formed a veil from the sun, the leaves of each just about out of reach of each other. This was called crown shyness, she had read, the founders were unsure why it happened here, within this community where togetherness was embedded within the foundation of the program. I guess, even when you're gone, your neighbours still annoy you, she thought.

Anyway
tomorrow she was bringing her daughter here for work experience. She would remind her which leaf she favoured, stitched strategically into the conversation. About how the rumour was that the veins of each leaf resemble those of your insides, but she knew her daughter would scoff and deem it a marketing ploy. Her

daughter, the flowering perennial, glancing at the leaves as she
herself grew tired, all of a sudden, as she had been doing recently.

Anyway

for now,

she did not want to think of home, as she
inhaled the scent of the forest, her brain registering hair lacquer,
perfumes, ashtrays and bubble gum.

She thought of the street she was raised on, right on this land, of
roller-skating into the road and narrowly missing her father's newly
washed car.

And as these woods now hummed for miles, at PLOT291 near
BIRCH38, she could have sworn she heard her name being called
in from the porch.

How you are using your time is not good enough.

Tailie

The man next to you has left the carrots
Which you thought was pretty obnoxious
Those carrots have come a long way to get here
From their humble beginnings.
You don't even like carrots, but you think they deserve a moment
to be tasted, so you eat them whilst he's asleep, his mouth hanging
open. They probably wouldn't have wanted to be inside his mouth,
anyway.

The woman behind you is coughing up a lung
All you can think about is that the air is recycled and that you're
going to catch whatever she has. Your nose is already starting to feel
blocked.

You've taken your shoes off because that's allowed here and only
remember when you're washing your hands in the appropriately
named water closet.

When the turbulence starts, no one seems to panic, apart from you.
You did not bother to read the safety information because you have
watched Lost enough times to know that you have a good chance
of surviving because you have a complicated back story and the
audience will want to see more of you.
You tell yourself this when the masks drop to calm yourself down.

You wonder if the airhostess has a very narrow house where she can only walk in straight lines. You're shocked that her hair stays so tidy as she's hurrying up and down the aisle. You make a note to book a trim when

When the pilot says 'Brace for Impact' over the intercom, people are dramatically following suit and part of you is proud that you are a trendsetter.

You hope that your ears have popped and that you're not underwater. Everyone knows you should wait half an hour after eating before going swimming.

You wish you hadn't had those carrots.

Blanket Fort

We built a blanket fort in the living room
Using the sheets you couldn't sleep under
Cloud watching stains
Shaped like mistakes, or goats

Placed party rings on fingers
Tips bitten to kindling
Watched *The Office* finale
And cried like widows
Fresh from a wake

We lay there for days
Playing Heads Up guessing games
Cracking jokes
Choking on the secrets stuck in our throats
Slept dreamless slumbers
Taking turns keeping watch

When the morning came
900 diagonal lines
Across days I couldn't name
We dismantled our citadel
Telling each other
We were too old
For castles made of quilts

Returned to separate beds
In separate cities
Closed our eyes
Counted to 100
And still couldn't find a better place
To hide

Snobs (is a sacred space)

There are two girls
in a single toilet cubicle.
One peeing, head resting
on the empty dispenser.
Possibly unconscious,
but still able to pee,
so maybe not.
She is wearing a dress
that she cannot afford to keep.
The label left scratching the mole between her shoulder blades
She'll take it back tomorrow; claim it didn't match the shoes.

The other girl is not as drunk, but is still pretty drunk.
She leans against the cubicle wall
A clean pair of pants folded up in the zip up pocket of a clutch bag
Residing in her sweat filmed right armpit
Because it's Saturday night and you never know.
She texts her ex
Even though
She knows

A hall

of records

or numbers

or spaces

still undone

Ruins

or relics

disciples

Second chances they don't ever matter
People never change
Once a whote you're nothing more

She shouldn't.
He checked in for pre-drinks
Four hours ago in a bar
Not too far
So she tells herself
This time
It might be different.

Outside a pack of boys
Who call each other lads
Who think that they're men
Wear coats
Because the cloakroom charging a £1 per item
Is a rip off
When a bottle costs the same.
It's easier to conceal insecurities
Under layers of clothing
Than powder inside socks.
The boys smell like sweat
But not good sweat
Like after sex sweat
But 'this shirt was left damp in your mother's washing machine
too long'
sweat.

Sorry that will never change

I just can't look it's killing me and taking control
Jealousy turning saints into the sea
Swimming through sick lullabies
Choking on your alibis

And I can tell just what you want

You don't want to be alone

You don't want to be alone

And I can't say it's what you know

But you've known it the whole time

Yeah, you've known it the whole time

They swarm the dance floor
Not dancing
Jumping
High
This is the only thing they know how to do
When they think they're being watched.
They resent the women,
Who know what its like
To be looked at
Who move like liquid between palms
Too quick to catch
And keep.

A bottle bottom is smacked on a rim
Beer erupts, sucked, downed, smashed
Slivers of glass
Pierce cheap soles,
Prod soft –

A girl in a crop top checks her heel
Handprint on the wall
Wet
A boy refers to cinderella on an improvised line.

I was bold she was over the worst of it
Gave me gear thank you dear
Bring your sister over here
Let her dance with me just for the hell of it

Big black boots
Long brown hair
She's so sweet
With her get back stare

Oh my friend
You haven't changed at all
You're looking rough
and living strange
And I know you got a taste for it too oh oh oh

Hey shady baby I'm hot like the prodigal son
Pick a petal
Eenie meenie miney moe
And flower, you're the chosen one

Puts his hand on her belly skin where her cat usually sits
She turns away
He calls her a tease
Stays where he is.
Feels her spine meet the wall,
her hair stick
She wishes her cat were here
To dig her claws, cling into his skin.
Because she just wanted to dance
In the dark
With strangers
Whose adolescences shared a soundtrack.
To stare at the ceiling
Watch the lights loop
Forget what's happening outside
Lift your chin to the air
But if you look a guy
in the eye
in a club
It means yes
So look down.
Apologise
She says sorry

(I gotta leave)
Get down girl,
go 'head get down
(I gotta leave)
Get down girl,
go 'head get down
(I gotta leave)
Get down girl,
go 'head get down
Get down girl, go 'head

Soft lips are open

Them knuckles are pale

Feels like you're dying

You're dying

To her legs
For being bare in this weather
and for the walk they'll have to do to somewhere not hers
Sorry to her stomach
For not eating the garlic bread she's been craving for a week
So she could wear this.
For her whole self
For not having the energy
or the experience
or the volume
to say no

Apologise
And pretend that it's for him
He might be satisfied with that.

The pack of boys all clamber onto one another
Ironically, like a washing machine load
She gets lost
Thank God
Snakes to the bathroom
Where
Seated girl opens her palm to her friend

And I'm singing 'oh oh'
on a Friday night
And I'm singing 'oh oh'
on a Friday night
And I'm singing 'oh oh'
on a Friday night
And I hope everything's
gonna be alright

I wish you'd stop ignoring me
Because you're sending me to despair
Without a sound yeah you're calling me
And I don't think it's very fair

I'm gonna fight 'em all
A seven nation army couldn't hold me back
They're gonna rip it off
Taking their time right behind my back

Hey I can be the answer

Who calls to the stall wall
A stream of toilet paper is chucked over
Like a white flag flying at a feminist rally
There are
Girls
No longer women
Young enough
To not compete
Instead share
Compliments
Help each other
Out of shape wear
Into heists
for free drinks
And that's it
Out there.

The sanctum empties,
Leaves Mary the toilet assistant
Enclosed by deodorants and lollipops
Provisions prepared by what it says is needed
in pre-teen magazines

I'm ready to dance when the vamp up
I fly like paper
Get high like planes
You were a child
Crawling on your knees
toward me
Making mamma so proud
But your voice is too loud
Run fast for your mother
And fast for your father
Run for your children
For your sisters and brothers
Leave all your loving
Your loving behind
You can't carry it with you
If you want to survive

And all the roads we had to walk are winding

And all the lights that lead us there are
blinding

There are many
things that I would like
to say to you

But I don't know how

But if you close your eyes
Does it almost feel like nothing changed at all?

And if you close your eyes

Does it almost feel like you've been here before?

How am I gonna be an optimist about this?
How am I gonna be an optimist about this?

If you close your eyes

Does it almost feel like
nothing changed at all?

She curses the puddle of pee,
now seeping under the door
Checks her phone's clock,
Knows that her children's
alarms will be sounding
in four hours
And she yawns--

On the dance floor,
The girls
move like women
Old enough to know better:
What they like,
These boys
who think they're men.
There is sweat
almost a shine
And songs sung with sore lungs
From the weekly repeated set list
Of parables
They all pretend
they know the words to.

Da Vinci

i'm not afraid to say that i find psychology difficult to understand
and even harder to spell
that i've spent lunar cycles
deciphering stances,
movements,
pauses
in
speech
because what we say and what we mean
might as well be poles on the axis of this conversation.

i've never been very good at confrontation
will orbit through awkwardness until this constellation burns out
instead, i've whispered words into pillows
folded into pages of books
and flattened into the silences between my favourite songs
(that i'm starting to think were written about this exact situation)
thoughts floating up into the atmosphere
without anyone there to catch them.

back down to Earth,
there's an Italian man with a beard
and a desire to discover the world above our heads
and beneath our skin
he pays gravediggers for bodies
dragged down alleyways in the dead of night
criminal curiosity
that'll keep you awake long enough that you ache to dream like him.
Da Vinci: the man of wisdom and wonder
dissecting others to find the reason for the sink in his stomach
and beat in his chest.

if i were to open myself up
slice my skin
break my bones
encase my hands into the parts of my person
that one slaved to keep me alive
i'd find subtle
sharp
recollections of your touch.
intertwined ivy between my ribs
forcing its way into the cement of my being
that i've spent decades building
but took you seconds to demolish.

what once kept us confined to this trajectory has shifted
a split second screen of static:
a blink,
a blush,
a jaw clench:
easily missed.
our fingers hold tan line ghosts
of what was once important enough
to alter our own landscape.
hidden in pockets
alongside
a thousand hour narrative condensed into
a sigh,
a shrug,
a hairline fracture left unseen
our names written mirrored so no one reads them together

i never realised how much of me
is really you

until my ribcage hollowed
and my heart yelled out
the whispered words inside pillows
unfolded from book spines
and sited between songs
that's where they'll find us:
as skeletons and in silences
trapped between chapters
and scattered amongst stars.

Amy and Tau have squatter's rights

The front door that needs three keys was left unlocked one night.
You're sure that you checked before you went up, but there is was,
slightly ajar, a draft creeping in.
Nothing was taken, thank God, or at least not anything detectable.

It was a redundant invitation anyway, the door left ajar, since they'd
been waiting in the loft insulation for years.
Amy and Tau came down the next day, no notice given. It should
have been obvious really, mirroring a badly written mystery saga
aired in the mid afternoon.
They bought a suitcase on wheels and a gym bag, barely enough for
a weekend away. They packed light. At first you thought they might
not stay long, but they just knew that they could rely on you for the
extras. You cursed yourself for taking the toiletries at independently
ran bed and breakfasts and told yourself it was karma.

They had started off being quite entertaining at parties, a source of
anecdote over half filled shopping baskets on your lunch break.
After all, Amy's feng shui business was really taking off; the flexible
working hours helped and people wanted to know about how it
was all going, just didn't know how to ask. The conversation mostly
focused on them instead. You didn't think they'd be impressed by
Amy's theory of leaving the hob on to heat the house up since the
report of melting ice caps came out. Plus your bills were mounting
up, so food stickered with the whoops labels would have to do and
you pretended you didn't notice when your friends stared at them.

To be perfectly honest, you wanted to say, they had become quite
malicious, restless, difficult to bear. You wanted to use the word
'destructive' about them, but knew that people who's biggest concern
was whether their chocolate spread had palm oil in it just wouldn't

get it, even though this was a valid issue to be worried about and you scolded yourself for being selfish as you ate the out of date lasagne.

One night you caught Tau going to the toilet in the dresser drawer that housed all of your old notebooks and all of your imaginary ex-boyfriends' names ran into each other and you cried like your heart had broken all over again. He told you he was sorry, but you could tell that he was lying, that he had never been in love before, even with someone imaginary.

You started researching Amy and Tau's species online. You highlighted a lot of words, which must have meant you understood them. The statistics were worrying, but so was the deforestation of the Amazon just for us to eat chocolate spread and the photos of the latter was more dramatic so your issues remained away from the headlines and budgets and you decided it was time to deal with this squatter problem yourself.

You moved Amy and Tau's bed into the cubbyhole amongst the coats, but this just gave them a concentrated territory and your shoes started being filled with eggs and receipts for items you didn't have time to return. Sometimes you put the shoes on without checking. You caught them conspiring about it in hushed voices, and when you confronted them, they tirelessly questioned your actions to the point you started to doubt yourself. You told yourself you can get through this. That you are the leading lady of your own life for Christ's sake and then remembered that this is a line from *The Holiday* and you really need to stop stealing other people's mantras. And talking to yourself.

You bought a 'for sale' sign in the newsagent's window and used persuasive language but didn't get much interest. There was that one phone call, but when you answered it was just someone breathing heavily down the phone. You realised that it hadn't rung at all.

You had been sleeping in the porch for some time now, found the electric meter more comfortable to lie on than a bed filled with eggs (you must stop buying eggs). Tau had locked you out a couple of times, made you late for work which made the vein in your boss' forehead throb but he knew by how your eyes were red that he couldn't say anything.

One day, when you had to work late, you saw smoke coming from the estate and you pretended to act surprised.
You knew Amy had been complaining about the cold that morning. That fire meant rebirth in some cultures and that's what they'd use as an excuse for the incineration.
You knew that really they were initiating you into their way of life. Turning you to ash so that you could look more like them.

You took this job because your own degree gives limited career choices

You took this job because of the holidays

You took this job because you leave at 3:30, right?

You took this job because those who can't—

off

wake up switches by the bed bedroom window closed feed cats
bathroom window closed tap on tap off grill on straighteners on
straighteners balanced on book shelf toast under bottom half
dressed toast flipped knife butter marmite knife in butter top half
dressed spread butter marmite grill off two switches grill left open
door closed eat scroll do not see what you are eating hair curled
straighteners off unplugged switch off balanced on book shelf caught
fire house on fire phone in sick its easier to lie pants on fire i can't
come in today sorry sorry sorry sorry sorry i'm sick i'm sick i'm sick
i'm sick i'm sick i'm sick i'm sick i'm sick i'm sick i'm sick i'm sick i'm
sick i'm sick make up on clean teeth tap on tap off bathroom
window closed door closed kitchen window shut grill off fridge
closed tap off door closed straighteners off bedroom window closed
plugs off straighteners off straighteners balanced on book shelf
bedroom door ajar living room windows shut plugs off cats fed
bathroom door shut grill off kitchen door shut straighteners off
balanced on book shelf window shut door ajar cats inside door
locked the lock turned you heard it you're going to be late door
locked the door is locked my eyes aren't wrong the words are not
wrong say it out loud off off off off off off off off off i'm sick but not
wrong no one is getting in time to go you're gonna be late sick late
sick and late sick and late sick and late sick and late sick and late
sick and late sick and late keys away walk past windows check they're
shut there's a gap there's no gap they could be on vent go back un-
lock the straighteners they're off they're balanced on the book shelf
inhale say 'it's off' you'll remember that way its off its off its off its off
its off its off lock the door push down on the handle push the door
the lock turned you heard it you heard it you heard it push down
push down push down push down push down push down don't turn back it's
fine you're fine you're fine you're fine you're fine you're
fine   you're fine

you're fine

Seating Plan

There is a girl at the back of the room
Shaded in red on data forms and her teachers' cheeks
Made up of curse words written in cursive
Who snaps borrowed rulers
Steals sharpeners for their blades
Heckles the new teacher for mispronouncing her name
Who can paint her face into a masterpiece of illusion
Leans back on her chair and dares herself to let go
Just so she can check if anyone would notice her noise
Unlike home

BSA

all the night to go
just take it as the siren
just the same siren
perhaps this, perhaps that
sort of a hunch that anything
could happen on
a night as this

      take the train into town
      before the tunnel
      envelopes you
      you can just make out
      the lettering
      at the entrance
      a memorial, almost

the one thing I had always
said would never happen

      there was no point
a pack of cards
      trying to piece people
they sound miles away
      back together
hang on and keep up
      they assembled parts
think of Margaret
      of a war
      that killed them
that torch I had always wanted
to throw away

cement poured
on top of them

half-light
   53
two souls
   trapped in that day
with a single thought
   deep down below us

put the kettle on love
my mouth's bone dry.

Octopus in a Jar

She peels away all the pith on a satsuma before eating it.

To describe it as flesh would be too cliché, the juice plump, almost sour, almost.

The pith gathers in her lap like remnants of war, like metal bent into shapes and buried.

Her fingers are mottled with ink, tattoo-like, as she pulls each segment apart; they do not darken.

*

Her butcher had a heart tattooed on his neck, the name in the banner blurred out. She'd come here fortnightly for the fish heads, a wink on the side for free, although she didn't ask for it, although, of course that didn't stop him. She carried the fish heads home, the bag swinging. She stepped over discarded tights, left behind by a woman she did not know, changing between men, emptying herself across her porch.

She would empty the bag into the biggest pot there was, the heads boiled down until the water was muddied with membranes and scales, the bones heavy at the bottom. Like any type of cooking, she knew there was a fine line between perfection and overdone.

She had really overdone it this time. There was a pasta bake planned for tonight that could have led to something finally happening with Steve but now everything smelt like fish, for fucks sake. The groan came from the depths of her housemates' throat, head tilted back like during an ascent of a rollercoaster, the rumble like gargling mouthwash without the mouthwash. It thundered across the living room through the kitchen door, followed by cursing, the harsh twang reminding her of home as a pang growled in her stomach, as 'why did you have to use my fucking pan when you have two of your own' filled the space, at which point she drained away everything but the skeleton, in her own sieve she'd like to add. She took a fish head between thumb and forefinger, wiggled the jaw, apologising with an eyeless echo, thought it was best to open a window.

She thought it was best to not let them dry on the radiator, so left them on a flannel, draped across her window ledge. Flannels are cheap, easily replaced, and this was before losing sleep over landfills was a worry and in a way there was a good level of irony in how she was taking dead things from the sea, preventing them from eroding, declared in front of the city as evidence of permanence far beyond the house they now lived in. She was learning that everything was a concept. They would dry out, the flannel tight and crunchy, the bones like jewellery, neat and declared.

For their trip, she enclosed the heads neatly in cotton wool, the type that comes in long folded lengths and made you clench your teeth as you unravelled it. They were transported in a bubble wrap lined envelope on her lap – reused from a present from her Great Aunt - as the bus engine juddered, she imagined the fish whispering to each other, excited about where they were about to go.

*

It had begun with Dennis.

Dennis was her sister's, but when he died she was too inconsolable to organise the funeral. She had taken it upon herself to be the undertaker, wrapped him in a sock she couldn't find the twin of, tail first, his nose poking out, his teeth almost smiling back, almost.

She placed him in a shoebox because that was what she'd seen done in films even though he only took up a tiny part of it.

She concluded with a 'see you soon, Dennis' as the family watched her shovel soil back over the box, and they thought it was a strange thing to say, but let it go because there was bigger things to worry about like next door putting their rubbish in their bin again and how they would confront them over this since 'the incident', not landfills or hamster life spans or whether their daughter was a psychopath.

A few weeks later, she checked on Dennis, who wasn't quite ready yet. Ready for what, she wasn't sure, but she told herself she'd think of something. Maybe something that involved glitter. She liked glitter back then.

*

When she told her future husband about her home-grown taxidermy habits over sea bass on their first holiday, she swears he put the ring shaped box back in his pocket. She mentioned this to him years later and he insisted that it didn't happen, although every time he opens the oven to check on dinner, he shouts "Dennis is not ready yet", and when dinner guests ask what he means, he says that he's forgotten the origin, probably something from the blurry years of art school.

*

It is known that tattoo artists practice on themselves before pigs' skin, before other people, the same bannered heart across three beings, unsure on what to write inside.

And she was wrong, it hadn't started with Dennis. That space in time when your memory is used to stock actions, like balancing or holding a pen or remembering your parents' faces, did not store her memory of swindling the tooth fairy.

She had saved her baby teeth, lined up in the felted ring section of her jewellery box, about to bite. This is what she had told her daughter, when she caught her running her chubby three year old fingers over the ridges, thankful she had inherited her curiosity, wanting to keep it intact, wrapped in cotton wool, an odd sock.

There's five minutes to go until the end of break and she's sitting describing the last hour, the excuses that had flaked apart in her front of her.

She recited how when she was their age, she had borrowed an octopus in a jar from the science department to draw over the holidays, that she'd carried it the two miles home, resting it on garden walls as she went, the suckers almost like open mouths, almost.

She had told them they were not resilient these days, instead impatient and lacking passion, full of complaint at dirtying their hands.

Her own pick the pith away, charcoal dim against the stark orange, a pip spat back into her palm.

How dare they not care enough about their craft, she says.

How dare they not love it to death.

wash your mouth out

the first, third and 784th time i do laundry
all of my clothes resurface as mixed berry teabags
as pink as insides
freshly born
i gather them up
unsure

my mom irons my dad's handkerchiefs
which seems like an unnecessary level of chore
the only way she'll stay awake during movie night
the board creaks, steam weeps
my dad pauses the screen and says:
"we're missing important plot points"

i ladder my school tights because i'm edgy
a boy calls it a stairway to heaven
so i superglue them shut
ask for trousers next term

i scrub bloody underwear wrung out in the sink
left crumpled
an animal spilled out
on the edge of the road

i have watched my red drain away enough times
to realise that
there is a part of me
that doesn't ask for permission.

i start collecting lunar wounds across my palms
from clenching my fists hard enough
to fight like a girl
(for air time in discussions
and i'm pretty sure i've had my hand up for a while)

i watch men have conversations like it's a competition
whereas women talk over one another, still listen
struggle for breath

puckered sentences let lose too quickly
hesitant
stack themselves on dirty plates
waiting
to be apprehended

i want to call it 'waste'
this muddy neglect of time
but i'm a hypocrite
i tell myself there is time
tomorrow, i will make

tomorrow, i will

but there have been too many tomorrows
there have been centuries of tomorrows
lost inside washhouses and at kitchen sinks
scrubbing the same thought over and over

i tell myself it is my duty to be dirty
i make mess
i choose not to clean it up

Mrs Tiggywinkle has fallen off the shelf again

Mrs Tiggywinkle likes tea with milk and ____ sugars and a biscuit.
Mrs Tiggywinkle's favourite colour is red because her birthstone is
a garnet.
Mrs Tiggywinkle sometimes likes to wear other people's _____.
Mrs Tiggywinkle likes music by Neil Diamond.
Mrs Tiggywinkle loves _____ fresh flowers in her room. Her favourite
are lilies.
Mrs Tiggywinkle will _____ at night time.
Mrs Tiggywinkle can _____ out sometimes but staff help her with
this.
Mrs Tiggywinkle likes to help set the table for dinner.
Mrs Tiggywinkle used to catch the number ____ bus. She likes to watch
the buses go past _____ her window.
Mrs Tiggywinkle enjoyed _____ and _____ at school.
Her handwriting was very neat.
Mrs Tiggywinkle doesn't talk much anymore but likes to listen.
Mrs Tiggywinkle has a sweet tooth. She likes to eat her pudding first.
Her _____ is trifle. Mrs Tiggywinkle has diabetes, so portion
control is important. Her drinks _____ be thickened.
Mrs Tiggywinkle can't _____.
Mrs Tiggywinkle liked to go shopping with _____ daughter and
pick up a bargain.
Mrs Tiggywinkle is visited daily by her daughter _____.
_____ will help to feed Mrs Tiggywinkle and takes her to
the garden.
Mrs T_____
_____.
Mrs Tiggywinkle has reduced mobility but still likes to walk a lot.

She can be seen frequenting the corridors. Sometimes she asks for
_____, sometimes for her _____.
M__T_____h_____
_____s_____.
Mrs Tiggywinkle used to go __ holiday to Wales. She had a caravan in
Dyffryn with _____ husband _____.
Mrs Tiggywinkle _____ cardigan. Mrs Tiggywin-
kle _____slippers.
Mrs Tiggywinkle's life achievement was _____ a mother. Also
shaking the Queen's hand when ____ opened the shopping centre.
Mrs Tiggywinkle sometimes likes __ hold hands.

Albatross

Through the wall
There is someone talking
Someone who doesn't live here
But speaks like he is home
I do not want to hear what he is saying

You come in and tell me that jungles take up only 6% of the Earth's surface
But are home to over 50% of wildlife and you look hopeful

I tell you that's because we've built cities everywhere and that this planet
is fucked
Because that's the type of mood I'm in

And you tell me
That the densest population of peregrine falcons live in New York City
Where racoons teach their babies to climb fire escapes
That macaque monkeys have learnt to steal from tourists
That a 3-day-old caribou can outrun an Olympic sprinter
That sloths only leave the treetops to poop

That the baby iguana got free from the snakes

And that the albatross will wait
For his mate
Until she's ready

Greenhouse Glasses

There was a man living in the greenhouse at the bottom of the garden.

His eyes were the colour of open waters, where waves are born and break far from the shore. The area where sharks hunt.
I told him this, and he told me a fact about sharks, which I have since forgotten.

He wore shirts unbuttoned low enough for the front to billow like a ship sail, puffing his chest out, holding his breath in. A fog constantly around his face, 60 a day, never a cough. His lungs must have been like vacuum bags halfway through a house, but he could hold a note whilst whistling for longer than the birds could.
I told him this, and he told me a fact about songbirds, which was also something about the Wright brothers, I think.

He carried a matchbox in his breast pocket stacked with dead bluebottles. He liked to line them up across the greenhouse workbench and watch the sun turn them from slate to sapphire and back again. He told me that the colour blue used to be confused with yellow – which seems impossible but I googled it and he was right – and that it was one of the last colours to get its name. That fact I remember. I promised him I'd use it in a poem one day.

His hands looked like tree branches, gnarled and knotted and just strong enough to hold up a home. Too large for his arms, like a Quentin Blake illustration. I would slip BFG quotes into our conversations, but he never got the reference, instead wrote his own stories about a war I couldn't pronounce. His handwriting was like sweet pea tendrils, curled and long and rebellious.

He chose his own name, the original faded like the boxer inked on his right forearm; shouted across hospital wating rooms and met with a pause. He respected white coats and intellect so behaved when he needed to. Although, he also had gasoline opinions and I'd hear him argue sometimes, unsure about whom with. He told me he once took a knife to a pillow fight that was organised by the washing line and I believed him, I saw the feathers afterwards. He told me that the best method to knock out an opponent is with a smile, so when I saw him grin I knew something was wrong.

He could peel an apple in one long coil, a trick I have only been successful at once.

We were different shades, the man at the bottom of the garden and myself. I was inside most of the time, germinating. When pushed away from the television screen, I would wander the garden, stroking the leaves, tempted to pull until I saw roots. I liked to pop open his prized fuschia's buds and he would tell me that I mustn't; that they aren't ready yet. It was the only time he raised his voice to me.

One year, I asked if I could take home the caterpillars that were gorging on it. He didn't look over, too busy finding the beach on pg 72 of an A-Z. (His eyes weren't what they used to be, littered with flotsam, but he liked to know where he was and where he could be within a four-hour drive.)
There seemed to be more caterpillars than numbers could count, as I scooped them into a jam jar and he knocked holes into the lid.

I was ready to be a mother, filled the jar with greenery and cauliflower stolen from the fridge. I watched them eat and tried to decipher their personalities, held them close to my chest as he told a story about caterpillars having green blood and I thought that was obvious, that he may be losing his touch.
In the house, I left the jar on the windowsill next to the pegs. I knew he might just be able to make them out from his chair, the smell of tomatoes pinching his nostril hairs.

Turns out, I was a terrible mother and forgot about them for a week or two. They formed chrysalises, hung and hoped to their Gods that they'd wake up again. Hope to Gods they didn't have to live in a nose grease smudged glasshouse afterwards, smelling strawberries but never getting to taste them. When I told him this – it was raining so I instead decided to phone – he told me caterpillars don't have Gods but that maybe one day I'd die and become one if I carried on forgetting about creatures I'd trapped in jars. He hung up and I lay awake that night, certain that I could feel my sides growing legs.

For the next week, I sat by the jam jar, watching the cocoons do nothing. I then went to checking every 20 minutes, because I decided that's what a good mother does, and 124 lots of 20 minutes later there was a tear. Agitated for air and open - more open than her curled up comrades ever would be - I took the jar down to the bottom of the garden, knocked on the greenhouse door, giddy at the accomplishment that I had no right to own, but the man was not there. For a second I thought the butterfly might have been him, so I tipped it out straight away, regretting not naming it as it escaped.

I found him in the hospital, with the wrong name above his head on a whiteboard like he was temporary. His eyes were rock pools reflecting the sky, too light to be a colour. He lay there, like a whale caught in the shallows with a belly full of plastic, his arms were pale and smooth like driftwood; he'd been away from the garden too long. I told him it was raining outside, that his plants would be happy for the drink. We talked about the colour blue again, about shade changing hydrangeas and soil with different levels of iron.

I crafted a strong handshake watching him say goodbye that day. I went home and wrapped his lawn in cling film just to watch the grass breathe, droplets forming across the surface. I let the fuchsia buds pop on their own accord. I fed his hydrangeas iron tablets and hoped that they'd change to his eye colour. I've started leaving leftover cauliflower cheese in the greenhouse, but the caterpillars get to it and it's gone before he gets a chance. I carry an empty matchbox in my pocket.

Inventory 3

- An ice lolly stick with the punch line bitten off
- A pair of false eyelashes, worn
- A pillow's worth of feathers, muddied with drool
- A bicycle bell shaped like Peter Pan
- The instructions to a flat pack wardrobe, splattered with blood
- A pencil sharpener shaped like a nose
- The foil wrapper of a Tunnock's tea cake, flattened
- The last page of the book you lent to me, ripped
- The first pair of Converse, pink, size 6
- All the passwords typed without the correct box being highlighted
- The branch that hits the top deck window
- A photograph of a firework display

Rough Terrain

look up
see the collage of stone
brick and glass
cut and stuck
with creases in the fronts
underneath
alleyway mazes leading to back to back courts
that patchwork the whole city
and never grow quiet
where ancestors share walls and woes and washday gossip
where we built bedframes
watches
buttons and guns
jack of all trades and master of none
does not apply here
a girl stamps out 1800 pen nibs a day
or she can find somewhere else tomorrow
the metal points shaped and sealed
doesn't know how to hold them when loaded with ink
sinks her hands into boxes of nibs
to cool down sore fingers still too soft for this job

look down
see the meadows become markets
where bargains are bundled in blue plastic bags
stacked high and shouted over
surrounded
in the rag resides riches
where we buy the ingredients of magic
flowers, fabric and food
make you believe this place could mend you too

watch your mother haggle and win
run your hands over textures
take it in
the flower lady
is offered a steaming cup of swilled out styrofoam tasting tea
no sugar, sweet enough
sits by her cart in all weathers
wrapped up in so many layers
you wonder how small she could be
to house lungs that can shout like that

look around
watch the shades of our skins
since the place was named
mix into a melody
aglow
we are the meeting point of mother tongues
the fork in the road to everywhere else
you thought you'd settle down in
until you met this one
a girl finds love in the symbolism she discovers at art school
spends days stalking the pre-raphaelite women
at their closed mouths and almost covered skin
she sees herself in them, they think
her family, who came here for her
hope she'd find her way safer than they did
in this second city
of second chances

listen
if what they say is true, about the lilt of a person and the
land where they lie
birmingham being born in a natural basin
makes sense
low and slow like a battery running out

like a phone conversation with grandparents
you wish you had paid more attention to
our voices have learnt to leap over
the heaviness of hard work
filling ears,
with metal
and market halls
of migration
to this middle land
to the heart

speak
loudly
we sound like a thousand years
of a thousand trades
spoken in a thousand tongues
because although moving forward
doesn't stop you from looking around
sometimes you forget to
take in all of this rough terrain
see what we've built together
imagine what we can do next

Apocalypse

If I am having a good day, it must mean that I'm about to die.
It can happen at any time, if the sun is out, the first pair of tights I
put on aren't laddered, the kittens haven't pooed on the sofa, the
photocopier at work doesn't jam
      when I'm putting through stapled double sided.
I've stopped walking under open windows or watching Harold Lloyd
films because I
      don't want to tempt fate.
"Miss, you look like the type of person to wait for the green man to
flash before crossing the road." I didn't realise that was an aesthetic,
until now.
We live on a flight path so every thirty minutes I'm reminded of my
own mortality
      and the fact that I recognise the underbelly of a Boeing 747
      more than the view from its window at 30,000 feet.

The problem with my 'fortunately, unfortunately' theory is that I
think your smile is
      going to be the death of me.
I haven't told you in case you stop laughing when I start
coughing blood.
Actually, for a while now, I've felt like everything is falling into place
for us.
Problem is, I think that this might induce the apocalypse.
Call me crazy, but I have noticed correlations between natural
disasters and our relationship status. Like that swarm of ladybirds
when we, well, you know.
Ever since we watched that Pompeii documentary and saw the
mummified couple
      found spooning, when you hug me in bed I swear that I
smell smoke.

Our freezer has stopped working so the snowball we'd saved from March has started to
> defrost and the cats don't drink it because they have better taste.

I walked past the war memorial on Spiceal Street and my name is on it, and I could
> have sworn it wasn't last time I checked.

The murmuration of starlings that welcome me home at 6:03pm on the dot, have
> stopped flying together. I tell myself there must have been a

falling out.

I'm preparing. I've done my research. I will no longer be the 'waiting for the green
> man' type of woman.

The first 72 hours are when most deaths by zombie bites happen, so I've worked out
> what we could use as weapons in each room of the house.
> (I reckon a toilet cistern lid to the skull would do serious
> damage.) The heart shaped stones we've been collecting
> on beaches make strong arrowheads, if only my arms were
> strong enough to be an archer.

I've been watching you butter your toast with a steak knife and reckon you're a little
> too quick to stab. I've been practising my embroidery on the
> bell peppers in the crisper drawer in case you nip an artery.

Talking of food, I don't think you've realised that I've started hoarding Loyd Grossman
> pasta sauce, not only because it's on offer and the Dolmio
> man gives me the creeps. I bought a book on 'foraging in the
> wild' from Oxfam and told you it was for a collage lesson
> with Year 9. I've made dandelion soup for your lunches this
> week. You comment on a faint smell of dog wee and I blame

the stock for being close to the sell by date. (It's also helped the lawn looks more conservative, which I guess will make the neighbours happy and less likely to eat our brains.)

You do the housework because you see that I'm preoccupied with 'my project'
and the clouds start rolling in.

For the more weather-based catastrophes, I've bought a foldaway kayak. I tell you
that I'm doing this as a nod to Chandler and Joey circa season 2 and I think that you buy it. I write 'oars' on the shopping list as a hint but you buy Quakers Instant Porridge instead and we eat it for dinner with sugar (for blubber) and ground flaxseed (for fibre). I guess, if push comes to shove, we'll use our forearms to steer, or might enjoy a float down the High Street since the leisure centres will fall into disrepair.

We binge watch anything other
than the news.

We have an argument over children since you see my search history about a 'DIY
papoose' and I don't have the heart to tell you it's for the cats, one on the front, one on the back. You pretend not to see the bulk buy box of non-lubricated condoms that I got a very strange stare at from Sandra on the till; athough I've read that they're good for slingshots or tying up the wrapped edge on a bag of pretzels when the resealable sticker gets fluff on it. I expect this will be the issue that sets you over the edge in the months to come.

The screens all turn to static so when you get drunk with the guys after work there's

> no way to track you down via GPS. When the buzzer groans
> at 1am, nocturnal me regrets not buying a gun, then I trip
> over the corner of the bed and dent my shinbone and decide
> that I should stick to archery. I make a note to get onto that
> soon, before it gets booked up with Katniss wannabes.

I open the door and there you are, a glitter-clad scarecrow leaning
haphazardly,

> pointing finger guns at me and attempting to wink.

And it starts to rain locusts.

When you're asleep, I spend my last savings on sending a swab of
our kiss spit into

> space, just in case we don't make it.

I tell myself I'll make the money back in tampons when cash and
coins no longer

> have monetary value.

The insects hit the window and the cats jump at the glass, hungry for
wings, preparing

> for their companion duties.

And when the storms don't stop, and we have to barricade ourselves
into the staff

> room of a multi-storey car park because the sanctuary
> password was a lyric I have always misheard, and there's
> raining blood and nuclear missiles flying across our town,
> we will just lie there like its Pompeii, and you will quote a
> vine, and I'll laugh. Like really, breath gasping, ugly cry,
> stomach stitching laugh and it will hurt a little, then a lot,
> and the sky will turn 'phone powering on in the middle of
> the night' bright, and I will just forget to inhale again, but I
> won't mind at all.

Onomatopoeia

They say that when you're out there
You can't see their faces anyway

He hoped that they were smiling
That they couldn't see the sweat forming on his top lip
He only has these three lines to show them

Hear the s   s   s   sss   stutter on each opening word

They say that a   second   long   Pause   feels   like   a

month

on   stage

He hopes that their silence
means they're hanging off his   every   word

Then it starts

A thousand slaps trapped in a rainmaker

Poured out before him

And his skin tries to remind him
What his father's palms feel like
But not now
Not in this moment

He pretends they're sending him Morse code messages

Sounded out

They say

You   are   loved

You   are   loved   You are loved

You are loved
You are loved

You are loved You are loved   You are loved You are loved You are loved
You are loved You are loved   You are loved You are loved You are loved
You are loved You are loved   You are loved You are loved You are loved
You are loved You are loved   You are loved You are loved
You are loved You are loved   You are loved You are loved You are loved

Dots

There are ladybirds living in your ceiling light
But she doesn't know that yet.
You're not sure how they got in with the windows locked.
You remember how she told you about her childhood
(You didn't know her then, but she likes to pretend that you did)
Building 'mini beast' gardens out of shoebox lids
Cut grass, dandelion heads, twigs
Making a home for something
That already had one
Forgetting that things with wings should not be trusted.

There are ladybirds living in your bath tub drain
But she doesn't know that yet.
She has read about it on the news
Mouths the word 'swarm'
Imagines her mouth full of scuttling
Thinks of Moses
Curses herself irrational but still
Writes the word 'plague' on her palm
And falls asleep with it against her cheek
So that she can brand herself as a bad thing.

You don't know how she got in with the windows locked
But she's placed a shoebox lid on her side of the bed
Cut grass, dandelion heads, twigs
Making a home for something
Thank already had one.
You decide that 3 will be your new lucky number
Like ellipsis,
Like good things happening,
Like the three small words spoken at the exact same time
As a ladybird settling on your tongue.

Glaciers

They say that if you want to see what a girl will be like when
she's older,
You should look at her mother.
Mine is short, smells of laundry dried outside
And her eyes are glaciers,
Waiting, calmly, to break you apart.
I am tall and I don't know how I smell.
My eyes are not glaciers,
Not even puddles of what she has seen.
Swamp Green. Toxic waste lakes.

I wear contacts because she once told me that I look better without
glasses and let me squint for long enough that it became a habit.

My mother is the reason that the most destructive hurricanes and
ships destined for sinking are named after women.

If there were to be a film of her life, my mother would be played by
Meryl Streep.
Emma Stone would play me, naturally.
My father would have one line that would probably be cut from the
final edit.
They're very different people, like how winter is a different planet
to summer.

They named me a palindrome, branded at birth to take three steps
forward and three steps back.
It's like they knew how I felt about dreaming big and reminiscing.
Nostalgic, pretend world, born in the wrong decade, past life, parallel
universe, different dimension.
They named me a palindrome, liked the sound of it.
Had a good rhythm with my surname; had Peaky Blinder blood.

I investigate my history, but my parents are planets and time is
different in outer space.
I ask them questions and get short answers.
I ask them questions and get a shake of the head.
I ask them questions: "Why are you so interested anyway?"
Our conversations become tides I'm too scared to swim in,
Find paddling up to my knees just enough to bear.

Three steps forward, three back.
I start checking for monsters under the bed.
Opening closets to expect skeletons, but find Narnia instead.

Because Swingler is a name that's survived blitzes and back to back
housing, Saturday derby scuffles and Snobs dancefloor.
A name entangled in a city of a thousand trades and a trillion
stories with a plot twist I definitely should have seen coming:
I find women.
Barlow, Yardley, Askey, Roach.
Women with good handwriting and favourite foods and laughs
that sound like mine.

Barlow, Yardley, Askey, Roach.
Women with bad eyesight but better judgement. Who squint
through swampy eyes so wear glasses instead.
Names above shop fronts and signatures that changed over night.
Daughters turned wives, turned mothers, turned off.

I find it difficult to imagine losing half of me.
Try standing on one leg.
Try chewing with only half my mouth.
It's impossible. But it happened. It's happening.
Daughters turned wives, turned mothers, turned off.
My ancestors are glaciers, melted into the sea.
Living in a landlocked city means we're just too far away to
reach them.

Barlow, Yardley, Askey, Roach. Swingler. Last one left.

I'll write your names within my poetry because I believe that once
you say something out loud, the words rise like smoke from a
forest fire.
From a secret cigarette out of your bedroom window,
From the kettle when she tells you she's leaving your home for his.
From the tail of a rocket destined for different planets.

I'll write your names across my skin, watch the ink seep in.
I'll think of you whenever I smell laundry dried outside or step in
puddles during rainstorms.
I'll become the reason that the most destructive hurricanes and
ships destined for sinking are named after women.
I'll do you proud, women,
Daughters, turned wives turned mothers turned ------

The Collector

INT: THE GREEN ROOM (The only room in the house named after a colour. The smell should be almost visual; smoke pirouettes from an ashtray, somewhere.)

MUSIC FADES IN - (Almost a 'coming of age' feel.)

PAN: SHELVES (The shelves are low enough to lie on the floor and read the labels, each inscribed with bubble writing felt tipped titles; stood slanted where comrades never made it home from the player, their ribbons wearing thin.)

TITLE CARD: 'THE COLLECTOR' (MAN 1 enters, eating a piece of bread and butter, the latter possibly stuck on some stubble. GIRL 1 is on the sofa, a dressing gown over her green gingham school uniform. MAN 1 promises to leave his collection to GIRL 1 when he passes, although she's not sure she'll know what to do with them all. Play Jenga with the boxes, unspool the ribbon and weave belts, make sun catchers out of the discs - apparently the post-electronic age will only bring boredom and craftiness. They used to be alphabetised, the titles, but now it's by date, which takes more energy to select.)

MAN 1:
Let's not watch the news tonight.

(MAN 1 never watches the news. MAN 1 only watches fiction; it's easier to swallow. He swallows the bread. In fiction there is foreshadowing that allows the viewer to be in on the trick; there's always a trick. If there's a twist that shocks you, however, then there's always the IMDB Trivia page to scroll through after the credits.)

GIRL 1:
We might miss something important.

(GIRL 1 knows she will hate watching every second of the news, but feels obliged to because she's a healthy and fortunate human. SHALLOW FOCUS: She watches as MAN 1's eye twitches, has noticed her own doing the same in shop windows when people don't thank her for holding the door for them, like a hint to a pre-emptive battle. This is not a battle scene, there is not even that much tension. The eye twitch shot was there to hint at a genetic relationship between the two characters, although will probably go unnoticed until read in the IMDB Trivia section.)

MAN 1:
I fancy a comedy tonight.

(MAN 1 always fancies a comedy. His expressions are better when creased up and howling, his belly warmed when held to stop choking. GIRL 1 does not like comedies because she feels it strange to laugh out loud in such a way. Also, there are always sexual innuendos, which are awkward to laugh at when you share a genetic relationship with your viewing companion, which she does. Alas, horror is never an option, fiction or not.)

GIRL 1:
Promise you won't stand in front of the screen and eclipse it then.

TITLE: FLASHBACK: POV SHOT: GIRL 1, on sofa.
(MAN 1 standing, blocking her view of the television, eating bread and butter, not blinking. She doesn't mind too much, the plot is usually easy to follow alongside her inner narration of overthinking. SHOULDER SHOT: GIRL 1 present day, on sofa. She wonders if MAN 1 sometimes feels the same, likes the act of watching something unfold and be refolded and fade and then you know it'll

be okay, because it can be, because it is on screen and sometimes real life isn't that different to fiction, but he just chews the bread instead, not blinking.)

GROUND LEVEL SHOT: MAN 1 takes a box from the shelf and reads out the title to GIRL 1 (inaudible).
(For once, GIRL 1 hasn't seen it before.)

GIRL 1
I haven't seen it before.

SHOT: CLOSE UP: MAN 1's eyes (There's a pause. Long enough to be noticeable, but not to say anything about it. He ejects the last tape, inserts the chosen one, and as it rewinds, there is no other noise in the room. The smoke continues to dance from the ashtray, somewhere.)

GIRL 1
No spoilers, please.

(GIRL 1 hopes the good guy will win in the end. She knows he deserves it. MAN 1's eyes are looking more tired, crumpled, and she's not sure it's from trying to match the laugh track's vigour).
ONE SHOT: GIRL 1 is still on the sofa. She's not sure she can watch him stand up for the whole feature, not blinking, waiting for it to unfold before him, waiting for the joke. ZOOM OUT, TWO SHOT, SHALLOW FOCUS: MAN 1 finishes his bread and butter. GIRL 2 joins MAN 1, standing, not blinking, her dressing gown too big. The cigarette burns out, as they wait for the tape to rewind.

muse

When she hangs a Renoir on her wall
And says it reminds her of you as a child
Pretend that you see it
One day you will

Listen to the songs
Written by men
Who say they find love in your eyes in the crowd
Where lights blind them
But do not crowd surf into their arms
Dance at the back
Do not learn the words off by heart
Or they'll stay there

Smile with your lips parted
Your crooked teeth are not the ugliest thing about you
Spend more energy learning your favourite sections of yourself
You were happier than it now seems

Take as many photos of yourself as you can
Decide on the angles that make you feel worthy of being preserved
like this
To be looked at by others
By yourself under covers

Adorn your wrists
With any other colour than red
Pile bracelets under school jumpers and reveal them between lessons
This is your first act of rebellion

Let yourself learn heartbreak
Piece yourself back together in kintsugi
Paint your cracks with gold
Hold
Until set

Know that suffering is not the only way to make masterpieces
Soak in the beauty of brushstrokes instead
The command of colour
Taught to you by vivacious women
Who see themselves in you
Drink their words until you're intoxicated
By the scent of their speech
Until you become their sister

Know that
You are not a muse
Lying bare and open
You are
Sunflowers
Exploded shed installations
You are a work of art, my dear
Sign your name in the corner
Let them look at you
And gasp

At the end of the night

She stations her impatience
On the mantelpiece
On a pillow
On a cliff edge
The frame full of hobbits and giants
She links my arm
Pulls me tight
Sorts her fringe
Finds her best side
The shutter clicks
(We thought the timer was on
So still count to six)
No one moves:
'Glasses off!'
Another shot
Just in case.

We reconstruct the image
At a different gathering
A homemade Colgate advert
Played on loop
We know the drill
There's no need for floor markers
The same set up and stances
Since her mom's mind grew darker
The wrapping paper is reused
Reused
Reused in separate takes
Changed angles and lighting
With stories told, paused
Repeated (now it's recording)

Instead of candid laughter
We're stuck with canned goods
Of American sitcom hilarity
Surrealism seeping into smirks
Like a finger on the lens
A picture speaks a thousand words
A strained smile won't shut up.

But as the flash blinds
We blink away our frustration
As these stills are stockpiled
Onto a gold-toothed time capsule
For taking her back when her own genetics
Start teething
So invite me to a slideshow showcase of a family
Now developed
Not blurred out by our own software just yet.

Here's a pact:
We promise
To not pull faces
That stick in the wind
Stuck in an album
Pages kissing
Pressed together in cupboards
Unopened since that year of winter
This complicated tangle of an extension lead household
Without much but a bloodline to stay knotted together
Saying cheese
(And pineapple sticks
Burnt pigs in blankets
Or a cup of tea in the nice china)
Are being kept warm
By mom's priceless kindling
And paparazzi habits

She has her evidence
That we were here
That we existed
That we had a good side.

I keep dreaming of

Community housing inside tree trunks
       Penthouse apartments the lift will not open to
              Shopping centre escalators and secret exit doors I find
without looking

                  Hotels with dark lobbies
                     Airport departure lounges
                       Holiday homes we've moved
                     to permanently
                Where the neighbours keep opening doors
            and slipping puzzles under the carpet so they
        leave the walkway difficult
      leaving riddles on the dresser
everyone is searching for my father
     who is standing right there
        about to pop out to do the lottery
         and each time I turn around
           our home is different
             and I can tell that I'm sleeping,
        I think
        My pillows at the foot of the bed
      And I'm standing with my hand in the letterbox
    Calling the outside in
Saying they can stay the night,
if they like.

Yet

Is

Grey coloured
The tour of the landing on a third date
The drawer of unsure belongings

Set in a doctor's waiting room
A pair of shoes left of a shore-side rock
A comma

Every rail in every charity shop
The mirrored cupboard door just before it shuts
The narrator's first intake of breath

The photo taken outside a bakery on its opening day
The owner grinning
Unsure of where to put his hands

"

Que   sera

                                    Sera

                                    Will

The   future's   no

Que   sera

Whatever   will   be
                    be

              ours
         To
                    See

         Sera

                    "

Hannah Introduces...

Jess Davies

Jess is one of my favourite poets. Their work welcomes you, works you hard, and then offers you a hot drink and a blanket at the end. It stays with you, like a friend. Their dedication and hosting ability at Stirchley Speaks is second to none, and I honestly don't think they realise how important they are to those around them. Performing on the carpet stage will always be a bright star in my life as a poet. Thank you. They make me want to be a better person. Oh yeah, and they're an unbelievable wordsmith. But you can see that for yourself.

Jess May Davies is an artist from Redditch, and is now a part of Birmingham's poetry community. Jess is the founder of Stirchley Speaks – a monthly spoken word night in Stirchley, and also a workshop facilitator. As a self confessed introvert, Jess uses poetry to explore their own identity in relation to mental health, environment and their own sexuality.

Jess also enjoys tea

Twitter: @JessMayDavies twitter
Instagram: @jessmaydavies insta

Facebook: @stirchleyspeaks
Instagram: stirchleyspeaks
Contact: stirchelyspeaktous@gmail.com

Even Attenborough Doesn't Know What's Going On

In the wild, baristas tend to perform well during the daily grind
however this specimen hasn't laughed at a single one of our jokes.

Instead she cracks a desert wide smile,
dry at the edges and already sinking into her bottom lip.

We ask for a coffee to go but she points to a sign that reads,
'We no longer cater to your disposable needs'
This seems rather emotional for a sign, but we take the hint.

At 3000ft below the surface of the silent treatment,
in the pit of her stomach -
Scans have shown a plastic bag of anxiety,
strangling the idea of a heart.

In a way never before seen on tv, or in real life
both ventricles have become infested with coral.
It must make it difficult to breathe
or to forgive.

She darts across the terrain,
from table to table, feverishly rescuing
abandoned coffee cups pushed close against her apron waist,
Potentially because she didn't have time to look for a tray,
or she is trying to resuscitate the meaning back into them.

She seems uncertain of how to do that,
Dragging what's left of our custom, out of sight
To be picked through and cleaned.
Some people might say she is over analysing what's left,

Projecting her personal life onto the inanimate objects in front of her
Its all very tragic
A store room littered with crushed pastry shells,
Scorned milk,
Cold tea left over from the last relationship to die in this cafe,
It fought for its life against a pack of wolves
that were never meant to be allowed in here
in the first place, something about historic wounds,
wailing teaspoons who just want to go home,
too many familiar faces outside,
no lipstick marks to reference
but there were faces pressed against each other,
Shared bed covers,
Jealousy over
remnants of touch,
How loneliness doesn't know how to hold her,
Is it even cheating
If it isn't exactly cheating?
Where are the receipts?
She wants a refund
she can't solve the thirst
Even in a paradise of beverages,
Hangover cures and regular routines –
She can't explain how it feels,
Here, we watch as she makes a bed of glass bottles at the bottom of
        the bin
Before extending her arm from a greater height –

It's all about to break,
Any second now.

Hannah Introduces...

Asim Khan

Sometimes, however you feel, you should turn up and try. I attended Brum Stanza night for the first time, tired but willing and was instantly enthralled with the power in the room. Asim's workshop piece stayed with me for days, his work is heartbreaking and real, and deeply intellectual. He is also the most humble of poets I have met, and I feel lucky to have met him and had the opportunity to gush about him. He is a hidden gem, and it seemed only right to ask him to feature in the book. Thank you for allowing me, Asim.

Twitter: @ecopoetic

Pareidolia

i was a thin boy when my mom took me to be exorcised. i had lost myself in a forest and had been followed back by bad thoughts. when i was shown the magic eye, i saw the face of an old woman, and i was asked if i knew her, but she did not speak her name.

/

in my childhood heart was a pain that had forced itself upon me against my will. faith, i was told could defend against the complaint, the denial of pleasure, the nights of unmapped sleepwalking. and in that dim room of rituals, i was given a ta'wiz; poetry in a locket, to ward off distress, whilst verses were blown over me, again and again: a mother's belief as a primary conduit to recovery.

/

after, during the morning prayer, my mind was empty. i went down-stairs and drew lines that resembled arabic on the back of envelopes, then watched from inside the hallway, the slender form of leylandii catching fire with the dawn sky. i was waiting for a new definition of grace to emerge, but my voice was broken, instead, only whistling the tune, i am not a thin boy, over and over. i was waiting for my body to feel full.

/

before breakfast, using the fridge magnets that held up the picture of my family on holiday, i spelt out a name. and when i had my fingers over the letters, i asked aloud for the last time if the name was cursed, and my fingers slowly slid, with the bowl of the 'a' replacing my body, and my thumb covering the frown on my face.

Hannah Introduces...

Hannah Ledlie

I had the supreme pleasure of working with Hannah (and making her be my friend) when coaching her during her second uniSLAM competition. Her poem 'Phone call' was met with standing ovation, both literal and in my heart. I am constantly in awe of Hannah's writing: her readiness to experiment and push the boundaries of what poetry is and of course, her wit. 'EMSPO' is my favourite joke a poet has made on stage. She is also incredibly kind and patient, and always shares her Subway cookies with the group. There is no doubt that Hannah is destined for incredible things. I cannot wait to see her soar.

Originally from Edinburgh, Hannah has competed nationally and internationally with the University of Birmingham slam team, as well as performing a number of solo sets around the West Midlands. She has also had success with her short stories, having been shortlisted for the BBC Young Writers' Award in 2015, and published in Ambit Magazine in August 2017.

Twitter: @hannahledlie
Website: https://hannahledliewriting.wordpress.com

sexcrime

in the unlight i lie in panic at my thoughtcrimes

                                            they are doubleplusungood tonight

        my thinkpol tries to knife them

                         but they flicker like the undark

            at the bottom of my blinds

            on the prolefeed joy couples have goodsex

i see goodthinkers have joy lives but i

                       bellyfeel ungood because

         i want ungood

             because her is–

i try crimestop

but can not

because her is–

no

if i ownlife   i ungood   i vaporised   i unperson

but her

but her

there are no words for

Hannah Introduces...

Dennis Nkurunziza

I have known of Dennis' work for some years now, but we only crossed paths properly whilst working on the same project with Beatfreeks during the Spring of 2018. Sitting in the Round Room at Birmingham Museum and Art Gallery, surrounded by works of art, Dennis' work still shone. His fluency, his tenderness, his ability to tell a story that makes each listener feel at home is what makes his work, to me, so special. It is soft, yet unbreakable. I am not surprised he is as celebrated as he is. Thank you Dennis, for the opportunity to spread your words.

Dennis is a final year mechanical engineering student at University of Birmingham who spends a lot of time experimenting with art and creative writing so he can improve his self expression.

Twitter: @dante_dmn

Mourning

We do not speak.
Instead, we begin digging further.
Re-visiting old wounds to find space for the new ones.
Dumping packed bags onto unsuspecting lovers.
We call this muscle flexing,
Unhealthy as it is.
We call this stage skipping,
Strong as it may appear.
We call this grief.

So we turn up the volume
Scream at the TV
Think about the times when Sir Alex was in charge.
We are used to sorrow weaving its way through our flesh
Powerful enough to be felt,
Yet the bleeding remains internal.
We call this suppression.

I have seen light leave my fathers eyes
When he spoke of the days spent under a bed
As bullets raced through the air to see who would find a mate first.
As the thunder they caused made him think of his brother.
Unable to shield him now that he was among those fighting the storm.
He called it war.

I see what it stole from him.
I understand what the bottle gives him.
I am glad we share the beautiful game.
I am glad we got rid of Moyes.
We continue watching,
Eventually we trade in our screaming for joy
Cheering as another game ends in victory
We call this bonding.
We call this love.

ACKNOWLEDGEMENTS

Thank you to my parents.

My mom, Wendy, the girl who didn't grow up. I have never known someone to be so strong yet so soft. Thank you for being ridiculously gorgeous in every way, for all the opportunities you gave me to shine across the years, and for still protecting your cuckoo baby from the storm. You are my rock and I vow to be as wonderful an adult as you. "I've been lost here before."

My Dad, Mark, my Popsicle, my favourite leading man. Thank you for teaching me about happy endings and believing in them when there's a plot twist. For reading the Rugrats books to me at bedtime and doing all the voices. For being the loudest voice in the house. For never failing to make me belly laugh. "Full?... Full? Of course we're not full."

My fangirls, Sev, Riba and Andi: for always turning up and telling me I'm good even when I'm not. For the laughs and the late nights on dancefloors and drivethrus – you are my sisters. My actual brother, Iain, for the awkward hugs and genuine care. Here's to 20p mix ups from Franks and the 'fake hand in the bed' prank: You've always allowed me to be weird, even though I'm annoying and embarrassing. Sorry about that.

To the rest of my family, without you, I would have no bizarre stories to tell. You are each absurd, you are each golden. (Including Jinkx and Rio, I never thought I'd be a crazy cat lady but you do have the cutest paws.)

To Stuart for always replying to the emails even when they don't make much sense. For the well-needed sass. For reminding me mush is for peas and not for poetry. For being the best publisher I could have ever hoped to have. Thank you for believing in my work from the get-go, even after the extensive pre-amble. Verve is beautiful; I hope you're proud of it, I know we all are.

To Luke for editing this chunk of consciousness. Thank you for getting excited about the group of cygnets outside of your office window, for loving potato scollops enough to explore their powers in a 5 minute sermon: you always remind me that everyone should be nice and distracted by the everyday. Thank you for teaching me the rules of the game, and for letting me play.

To Casey Bailey: my agent, my partner in poetry, my friend. You are an inspiration to all. I wish you were my maths teacher when I was at school, (but let's face it, we'd never get any work done). Thank you for always believing in my work, and telling me to RELAX. Thank you for helping me grow. I'm sorry I spilt that hot chocolate in your car.

To Hannah, Jess, Dennis and Asim: your poems are the show-stoppers in this book and I am honoured to house them here. You are wonderful poets and people. Thank you. Thank you. Thank you. Thank you.

To all those connected to the Brum poetry scene. To Amerah for her faith in me. To Jas for the first workshop. To Beth, Jess and Callum for the first feature. I have found my team and we are unstoppable.

Speaking of unstoppable teams, my UniSLAM family: Sean, Anne, Hannah, Mikey, Kim: Being able to coach you during uniSLAM changed my life and I am so proud to call you my friends. Here's to party rings and hummus and practicing over and over again. I can't wait to see what we do next.

To Toby and Vanessa for letting me sob on the steps at CUPSI. For picking me up and telling me my story is worth listening to.

To my Atherstone Theatre Workshop family: Dawn, Joyce, Becca, June, Eileen, Cathy, Maggie, John, all the young members. As a member, thank you for allowing me the space to explore who I was, on stage and off. As a leader, for letting me write and direct and being so supportive. It was an honour to tread those boards with you. I miss you every Tuesday night. To Walden. You're right, your woods are magical. To the sign and back.

To all the women who taught me at CTC, thank you for being such role models. I hope that in my work, I do you proud. Janine: I'm sorry if the grammar is terrible.

I always wanted to grow up and get excited about going to work each day. To all in the Challoner community, thank you for making my everyday extraordinary. Jo, thank you for your mentorship and your ferocity: the art department is so successful because of your dedication to it. I couldn't wish for a better place to teach, to perform everyday to a room full of young people who I try to teach and who sometimes compliment me on my outfit. Kids, you give me hope. I also get to draw a lot, which is super fun.

To Jack, my biggest fan, my albatross, my constant. Thank you for your unfaultable love and glorious light. And for always cooking the dinner. I could have lived a dozen past lives and still do not deserve such a soulmate. I love you. Thank you.

To every person who bought this book. I hope you crack its spine, highlight the bits you like, write in the margins. Enjoy!

ABOUT VERVE POETRY PRESS

Verve Poetry Press is a new press focussing initially on meeting a local need in Birmingham - a need for the vibrant poetry scene here in Brum to find a way to present itself to the poetry world via publication. Co-founded by Stuart Bartholomew and Amerah Saleh, it will be publishing poets this year from all corners of the city - poets that represent the city's varied and energetic qualities and will communicate its many poetic stories.

As well as publishing wonderful collections from poets with local links, such as Casey Bailey, Nafeesa Hamid, Leon Priestnall, Rupinder Kaur and Polarbear, we will also work with other poets who have close connections to our sister festival, Verve. Our Experimental Pamphlet Series, our poetry show collection from Matt Abbott and our anthology with Lunar Poetry Podcasts all fall on this side of our activity.

Like the festival, we will strive to think about poetry in inclusive ways and embrace the multiplicity of approaches towards this glorious art.

So watch this space. Verve Poetry Press has arrived!

www.vervepoetrypress.com
@VervePoetryPres
mail@vervepoetrypress.com